AROUND THE WORLD

ITALY

First published in 1997 in the USA by
Thunder Bay Press
5880 Oberlin Drive, Suite 400
San Diego, CA 92121

ISBN 1 57145 082 3

Library of Congress Cataloging-in-Publication Data available upon request

Editions of this book will appear simultaneously
in France, Germany, Great Britain, Italy, Spain
and Holland under the auspices of
Euredition bv, Den Haag, Netherlands

Translated from the French by Tony Burrett
Typesetting: Buro AD, Amersfoort
Printed by AUBIN IMPRIMEUR, Poitiers, France

AROUND THE WORLD

ITALY

Noël Graveline

THUNDER BAY
P·R·E·S·S

INTRODUCTION

At the mention of its name Italy excites the imagination in a way that few other countries do. In fact, not a single western country can claim it owes nothing to this nation that was the mother of men and cities, of the arts and the law. Italy, one of the most civilized places in the world, was nonetheless one of the last European nations to achieve unity. National consciousness on the pensinsula, as perceived from the outside, had become no less strong than it had been since ancient times and Italy owes this, above all, to geographical factors. Italian unity clearly results from the remarkable simplicity of its natural frontiers, which are formed by the summits of an arc of Alpine mountains and the coastal contours of the peninsula. The two largest Mediterranean islands, Sicily and Sardinia, are also part of this country. The whole tends to form a perfect link between Europe, Africa and the East. This does not prevent the Italian landscape from demonstrating a remarkable diversity and fragmentation, however, ranging from the glaciers of the Alps to Sicily, foretaste of Africa, while the ancient division between the continental North and the Mezzogiorno peninsula plays a greater role than ever before.

The traveller notices immediately within these well-defined frontiers how the State blurs into the twenty regions of which it consists and which are in harmony with natural realities. The three principal geographical elements of Italy are the Alps, the plain of the river Po and the Apennine chain, and correspond with numerous regional nuances, easily perceptible in the landscapes, and reinforced by the history, traditions and economy.

The Alps are often thought of as a barrier, but they are more a solid anchorage linking Italy to Europe, because the main routes from the continent cross a chain of passes which have been traversed since the dawn of time. In modern times the Alps have augmented their role as a castle of water above the plain of the Po, holding enormous reserves of hydro-electric energy. Different chains can be distinguished in the Italian Alps. In the west the Piedmont Alps, falling steeply to the plain, form a fortress whose ramparts rise to the 4000 metres of Gran Paradiso, Cervin and Mont Rosa. Of the valleys which converge into the Po, only the basin of the Dora Baltea diverges to form the Val d'Aosta.

Between the Simplon and Adige the Lombardy Alps are even more magnificent because they are duplicated to the south of the limestone Pre-Alps. On the Swiss border they form high massifs such as the Adamello, the Ortler or the Bernina, which feed almost two hundred glaciers. Ever since the Ice Age, these glaciers have extended to where the Alps descend to the plain and wherever an obstacle forced them to grind out a valley, today lies one of the lakes which have made northern Italy so famous. Some have been incorporated in the Pre-Alps, such as Lake Orta, Lake Iseo and Lake Como. Others, like Lake Maggiore and Lake Garda, lie in the plain between moraines. In any event, their waters exercise a beneficial effect on the climate, promoting the culture of wine and the establishment of dream gardens, which has encouraged tourism since the Age of Romanticism. In the eastern Alps the chains are broader, though the summits are not as high, and limestone dominates every landscape. This is striking in the Carnic Alps and the Pre-Alps of Friuli which extend the Karst region by impressive ravines and canyons. But the Dolomites are even more striking. This region was formed of a remarkable limestone rock which erosion has hacked, as if with an axe, into surprising and picturesque landscapes which attract just as many tourists as Venice. The plain of the river Po is closely linked with the Alps as a whole and

forms a notable exception in an Italy where the few plains are both coastal and narrow. Well irrigated, this plain is the country's prosperous garden and, at the same time, its most important industrial entity, built round dynamic cities such as Turin and Milan. The Po plain plays a vital role in the Italian economy.

The third fundamental element in the geography of Italy, the long, young Apennine chain, forms the sharp spine of the peninsula and runs from the region of Genoa, where they merge with the Alps, to the strait of Messina, where the Aspromonte slopes fall almost two thousand metres. These mountain chains divide lands with very different climates and lifestyles and for a long time formed an obstacle between the Tyrrhenian and Adriatic slopes.

Outside this simple schema, the Apennines manifest themselves in a great geological complexity which has led specialists to compare them with a badly-paved road. To put it another way, the Apennines change from the marbles of Carrara to the limestome plateaus of Umbria and the granites of Calabria, taking in the volcanic manifestations of Latium and Campagna.

It is necessary to evoke Sicily, Sardinia and the smaller islands, without which Italy would not be the same. Under the tall shape of Mount Etna, Sicily illustrates the transition between the Apennines and the Atlas Mountains of Africa while Sardinia differentiates itself from the rest of Italy, being part of the old continental shelf. As far as the small islands are concerned, certain of them, in the Campanian archipelago or Lipari, emphasize through their volcanic activity the intense underground activity which shakes the south of the peninsula; while others, far from the popular tourist routes, perpetuate ways of life which elsewhere have disappeared.

Finally, it should be remarked that despite the development of her coastline, Italy has not been particularly favoured with natural harbours and that her great commercial and maritime successes have only been made possible by an enormous amount of hard work. Although in general they are hostile to sailors, the coasts, in contrast, have proved eminently suitable for tourism and the modern age has witnessed the development of countless seaside resorts.

History usually comes after geography but the history of Italy is so complicated and overburdened with details that a brief glance must suffice. From the 8th century BC, when Rome was founded, until the fall of the eastern Empire in 476, this history is that of Roman civilization. In the Middle Ages, Italy was the stage on which the rivalry between the great European powers was played out, a rivalry in which the papacy played a role; and in the absence of unity was formed of city states and corporations. The Quattrocento, an amazing intellectual and artistic development, took place in the most troubled century of the country's history before the Renaissance established the influence of the Italian soul.

For many centuries the peninsula saw the passage of foreign armies, until in the middle of the 19th century a strong nationalistic sentiment emerged. In 1870, this 'Risorgimento' was crowned by the achievement of Italian unity and the naming of Rome as the country's capital city.

The result of this is that provincialism (here it is known as 'campanilism') is the most characteristic trait of social and political life in Italy. This parochial mentality rises above chauvinism, something that is illustrated, for example, by the fact that every big city has its own daily newspaper. Still more striking is the rivalry which reigned in the time of the Renaissance between the '100 cities' of the Po plain, where markets and festivals succeeded one another, to the great joy of visitors.

The combination of these physical factors and this history in well-known stages, however, is not enough to explain Italian genius. This genius, which the West has so much to thank for, and which makes every journey to Italy a sort of pilgrimage to the source, evidently springs from the Italians themselves. Scarce in natural resources the soil of Italy, in effect, has given birth to a singular people. Since time immemorial, the country has seen the greatest saints and the worst tyrants, the most enlightened spirits and the most destructive follies, champions of right and justice and the most cunning princes. Italy, one understands, has found wisdom and sparkles despite all the passion.

Direct heirs of an incomparable past – UNESCO have concluded that almost half the cultural riches of our planet can be found in Italy – the Italians are also very close to a history that inclines to scepticism, even cynicism. From this stems their paradoxical personality: inventors of idleness, these people are also the most active of Europeans, authors of an economic 'miracle', always cited as an example. Pioneers of democracy and elaborate forms of government, they sometimes show a pathetic face of politics and the State, yet always make tolerance a cardinal virtue.

In love with beauty, they have preserved the centres of their cities remarkably well, although at the same time they allow progress to deface the outlying districts.

Regarding beauty, the prevailing impression – happily – is that modern Italian creativity has no need to be envious of the past. In this age of industry has not 'design' been invented in cities which were already famous during the Renaissance? Cannot the talent of the builders of the alpine motorways, that blend so beautifully with the landscape, be weighed against that of the builders of the Roman aqueducts? While Ferrari is a byword in its field, and so dear to Italian hearts, cannot Milan compete with Paris as far as fashion is concerned? And what can one say of the Italian cinema, which has succeeded in making the genius of this people universally known?

GENOA

The houses of Genoa descend in serried ranks to the port which has always been at the centre of its existence. It could be no other way, because Italy's premier port is enclosed inside an ampitheatre of steep mountains. To the picturesque steps, hanging gardens and palaces which form the charm of the old quarters, in the modern era the capital of Liguria has added audacious routes of communication to the hind its facades treasures are concealed. The Town Hall, the ancient palace of Doria-Tursi, for example, has Paganini's violin and letters from Christopher Columbus. Further on, the Bianco Palace houses a museum of art while the Rosso Palace is also an art gallery. At the foot of the town, ancient alleys lead to the church of San Mateo, perfectly Genoese in appearance, whose crypt contains the tomb and sword of Andria Doria. Less famous than

Top: The piazza Corvetto.
Above: The church of San Mateo.
Opposite page: The Town Hall, Via Garibaldi.

Following pages: The port of Genoa.

interior. No less impressive are the harbour installations won from the sea while the concrete towers of its business quarter resemble a small Manhattan.

Nicknamed the 'Superb' or the 'Proud' since the 18th century, Genoa assuredly still merits this title today, and the via Garibaldi is the best illustration of this. Laid out in the 16th century, this highway, lined with palaces, is one of the most beautiful in the pensinsula and be-

this great sailor, than Paganini or than the discoverer of America, but also dear to the hearts of the Genoese, the patriot Giuseppe Mazzini, also a son of the city, looks out over the piazza Corvetto, one of the great urban squares.

THE LIGURIAN RIVIERA

The term 'Riviera', wrongly extended to other seaside resort regions, only applies to the Ligurian coast. All along the coastal arc the sun shines, the steep fall of the southern Alps and the Apennines protect it from continental influences and guarantees climatic conditions even better than those of Naples and comparable to those which prevail in Sicily. To the west of Genoa and its industrial extensions which reach as along the length of the via Romana, successor to the ancient via Aurelia. Further on prestigious San Remo, capital of this Riviera, is well-known for its flowers and palms which can be seen along the corso Imperatrice. In contrast to Genoa, the Levant Riviera is very wild, and the road twists and turns. The tortured landscape gives the picturesque fishing port of Portofino its charm. This port has become one of the world's most important tourist resorts.

Above: Bordighera.
Left: Portofino.
Below: The corso Imperatrice in San Remo.
Opposite page: A villa in San Remo.

far as Savona, the Ponent Riviera rivals the French Côte d'Azur in numbers of tourists, each of the small former harbours having become a seaside resort coupled with a marina. The economy of this sunny region has benefited from flower growing, as can be seen from the scintillating colours on the terraces of the very steep hillsides. The first great resort on the Ponant Riviera is the frontier town of Ventimiglia. A little further along is Bordighera, famous for its carnations and date palms and for the luxurious villas

*Above and opposite page: Two views
of Manarola, clinging to the steep
slope, one of the five colourful
villages of wild Liguria.*

THE CINQUETERRE

Riomaggiore, Manarola, Corniglia, Vernazza and Monterosso al Mare are five colourful villages wedged into the steep coast between La Spezia and Levanto at the extremity of the Levant Riviera. Known collectively as the Cinqueterre, they appear to be a challenge thrown down by nature in that their proximities seem infertile, whether for agriculture or fishing. Working generation after generation, however, the inhabitants of this savage Ligurian coast have tamed by force the steep slopes and created dizzying terraces where they cultivate the vines which produce the famous 'sciacchetrà' white wine. The fishermen of Cinqueterre were no less industrious and have often found ways of using the rough rocks to shelter their little boats. For a long time the villages remained on the fringes of tourism on the Riviera because no road worthy of the name reached them and according to circumstances visitors used a mule track, an acrobatic railway or the maritime route.

Today a corniche links the Cinqueterre with the Ligurian coast and it is easy to appreciate its charms and traditions and its wild environment. Each of the villages has an interesting miniature church and an architecture which exposes the sun and the landscape at one and the same time. But each village also has a character all of its own – Corniglia, high and remote; Monterosso, friendly and even having a beach; the other three having variations on a 'marine' theme.

PIEDMONT

It was history rather than geography which created Piedmont and which forged the identity of this region between the Alps and Apennines. Although its ancient capital Turin, situated in the centre of the plain of the Po, has always been influential, the unity of Piedmont was created around the mountains and the men of the mountains, under the protection of the House of Savoy. This makes even more remarkable the fact that Piedmont was the birthplace of the struggles for Italian unity.

Evoking the real mountain in this region is to speak only of the cramped valleys leading to the alpine passes which control the Piedmontese because the Italian slopes of the chain do not form a narrow, steep wall.

In contrast, in the Apennines, and most particularly across the peaceful hills of Montferrat, an original civilization developed, renowned for the making of two prestigious products – Asti wine and gorgonzola cheese.

Above the plain of the Po, the Alps sometimes begin in a range of foothills and it is on one of these, Mount Pirchiriano, that one of the most famous abbeys in Italy, the Sacra di San Michele, was built. On a pinnacle of rock long dedicated to the saint, the Benedictines erected their abbey in the year 1000 AD and there they prospered so well that two centuries later they held sway over one hundred and forty monasteries. At the end of a long staircase, one can admire a sanctuary in Roman-Gothic style, decorated with Renaissance frescos.

Top and above: The Sacra di San Michele, one of the most famous abbeys in Italy, built in 1000 AD. Opposite page, top and middle: The mountainous countryside of Piedmont.

TURIN

Well ordered, modern and dynamic, Turin corresponds perfectly to the image one has of the capital of the European motor industry. But if one looks more closely, one discovers that the city is elegant, lively and cultivated. Durably linked to the House of Savoy, which gave its kings to a fledgling Italy, Turin exhibits the pride of capitals where one can admire the Madame Palace and the Royal Palace, and preserves a legacy well worthy of a city whose central layout closely follows that of Roman times.

The vivacity of Turin life is centred around the piazza San Carlo, pleasantly bordered by galleries and arcades, and traversed by the via Roma, which emerges between the two twin Baroque facades of the churches of Santa Cristina and San Carlo. In the centre of the square is the equestrian statue of Emmanuel-Philibert of Savoy, his sword back in its sheath, after having vanquished the French at Saint Quentin in 1557 and so recovering his States after a twenty-five year absence.

Turin is a wonderful city for lovers of museums. The palace of the Academy of Sciences houses two exceptional collections, and the Egyptian Museum and the Galleria Sabauda are dedicated to painting. The Madame Palace houses a Museum of Ancient Art, the Royal Palace contains the historic arms of the Armeria Reale. The Carignano Palace has the interesting Risorgimento Museum. These are only the principle museums – to which must be added the rich Carlo Biscaretti di Ruffia Museum of the Automobile.

Top: The Via Roma.
Above, left: The piazza San Carlo.
Above, right: The Automobile Museum.
Opposite page: Equestrian statue of Emmanuel-Philibert of Savoy in the piazza San Carlo.

THE VAL D'AOSTA

With Mont Rosa, the Cervin, Mont Blanc and the Gran Paradiso, are the illustrious eternal snows which surround the Val d'Aosta, the smallest but the most mountainous of the Italian regions. Below these protective giants stretch thick pine forests and below these the flowering pastures which are at the heart of the valley's tradition of animal breeding and the manufacture of Fontina, an excellent fondue cheese. Despite the abundance of timber, which elsewhere has inspired an active body of craftsmen, the houses of the Val d'Aosta are of stone, including the roofs and only the balconies are evidence of the skill of the local carpenters.

The turbulant Doire Baltée is the principle axis of the region and, together with the torrents which con-

Above: The medieval chateau of Sarre, near Saint Pierre. Right: The chapel of the chateau of Fenis. Opposite page, top and bottom: The Gran Paradiso, in the region of Cogne.

verge into it, it commands the great routes to France and Switzerland, that is to say the Lesser and Greater Saint Bernard passes, while the modern era has seen the building of a tunnel under Mont Blanc between Chamonix and Courmayeur. This is why the town of Aosta, an important stage on the road of the Gauls, contains a number of Roman monuments, while the peaks of the valley have seen the building of defences of hundreds of castles, citadels and signeurial residences representing every period from the 12th to the 19th centuries. Near Saint Pierre, King Victor-Emmanuel II loved to stay in the medieval chateau of Sarre, at the gates of his hunting territories which he closed to create the wildlife sanctuary of the national park of Gran Paradiso.

LAKE MAGGIORE

"There was not a breath of wind there... One heard the slow and languid stream breaking on the pebbles of the sandy beach..." Like so many other romantics, musicians, painters, poets and writers, the great Alessandro Manzoni was bewitched by the fascination of Lake Maggiore. The most famous of the lakes of Lombardy is a universe in itself, which commences in Switzerland, fed by the Ticino, and whose waters who once ruled this region. Three of them are notable. Not far from Pallenza, the large Isola Madre is covered by an extraordinary garden of flowers and exotic plants which indicate the gentle climate of the region. Very close to the other shore, Isola dei Pescatori guards its traditional cachet around a fishing village which artists have made their own. Finally, the island of Isola Bella was chosen in the 12th century by the ducal family who had a

Top and above: The statues of Isola Bella.
Opposite page: The terraces and gardens of Isola Bella.

gradually change from jade green to deep blue as it moves to the south. At the same time, the severe Alpine grandeur gives way to an enchanting harmony evoking the Garden of Eden, particularly where the lake widens in its centre, with the refined resorts of Stresa and Pallanza lie on opposite shores.

The perspectives of the lake are complemented by the presence of the five Borromees islands which perpetuate the name of the princes great palace there. In Lombardy Baroque style, this residence is built above a series of 'caves' decorated in pebblework, which open onto the dream gardens leading to the lake through ten terraces populated with statues and rare trees.

Previous pages: The isle of San Giulio in Lake Maggiore.

*Above and opposite page right: The
Villa Carlota in Tremezzo on Lake
Como.
Opposite page middle: The Villa
Margharita.*

LAKE COMO

With its three long arms, Lake Como embraces some of the most seductive places in Lombardy, here discrete, there worldly, unpretentious villages and harbours alternating with villas of extreme refinement. Como, the capital of these shores, is a large town proud to have been the cradle of the Lombardy style graced by its "maestri comacini" who were at one and the same time masons, architects and sculptors, spreading their knowledge over much of Italy and its neighbouring countries. The town's shrines are models for this school, whether they are for Romance, Gothic or Renaissance art.

Despite all this, on the banks of Lake Como the attention is more readily drawn to the architecture of the resorts and to the gardens which accompany them. Among these, situated in a lovely position, is the town of Monastero de Varenna and the huge villa d'Este de Cernobbio, transformed into a hotel. More beautiful still, between the resorts of Lenno and Cadenabbia, sumptuous estates and their parks follow one after another without interuption on the Tremezzina, which was said to be the garden of Lombardy. The pearl of these, the villa Carlotta, in Tremezzo, is famous for the works of art it contains and for its garden, which has remained intact since the 18th century.

MILAN

The dynamisn and development of Milan is reflected in its concentric rings and in its boulevards. These enclose the famous marble Dom, masterwork of the flamboyant Gothic style, and its surrounding medieval quarters; then the inner suburbs built since the Renaissance, then belts of modern extensions surrounded by the constant traffic of the autostrades. Having the second largest population of any Italian city, the capital of Lombardy takes first place in economic activity. This has been so since the time of the Viscontis, then the Sforzas, who wanted to impose the grandeur of their capital on the rest of Europe. Milan was actually the source of the glory of the Renaissance, and still today the city exercises great artistic influence. Symbol of a vitality which says the Milanese never sleep, the celebrated Galleria Vittorio Emanuele ends, in contrast to the

Above: The cathedral of Milan.
Right: The La Scala Opera House.
Opposite page, top: The church of Saint Mary of the Graces. Below: The Navigli quarter.

Dom, in the illustrious theatre of La Scala, incomparable pinnacle of the lyric art. The heart of Milan is overflowing with incomparable treasures and it would take days to describe the collections of the Ambrosian Library, the Brera Art Gallery or the Sforza castle, not to mention the principal museums. There is also an abundance of monuments, bearing the very greatest signatures; that, for example of Bramante in his church of Saint Mary of the Graces, whose refectory contains Leonardo's Last Supper. Happily, Milan's grandeur does not exclude the picturesque, as can be seen when walking through the Navigli quarter of the city.

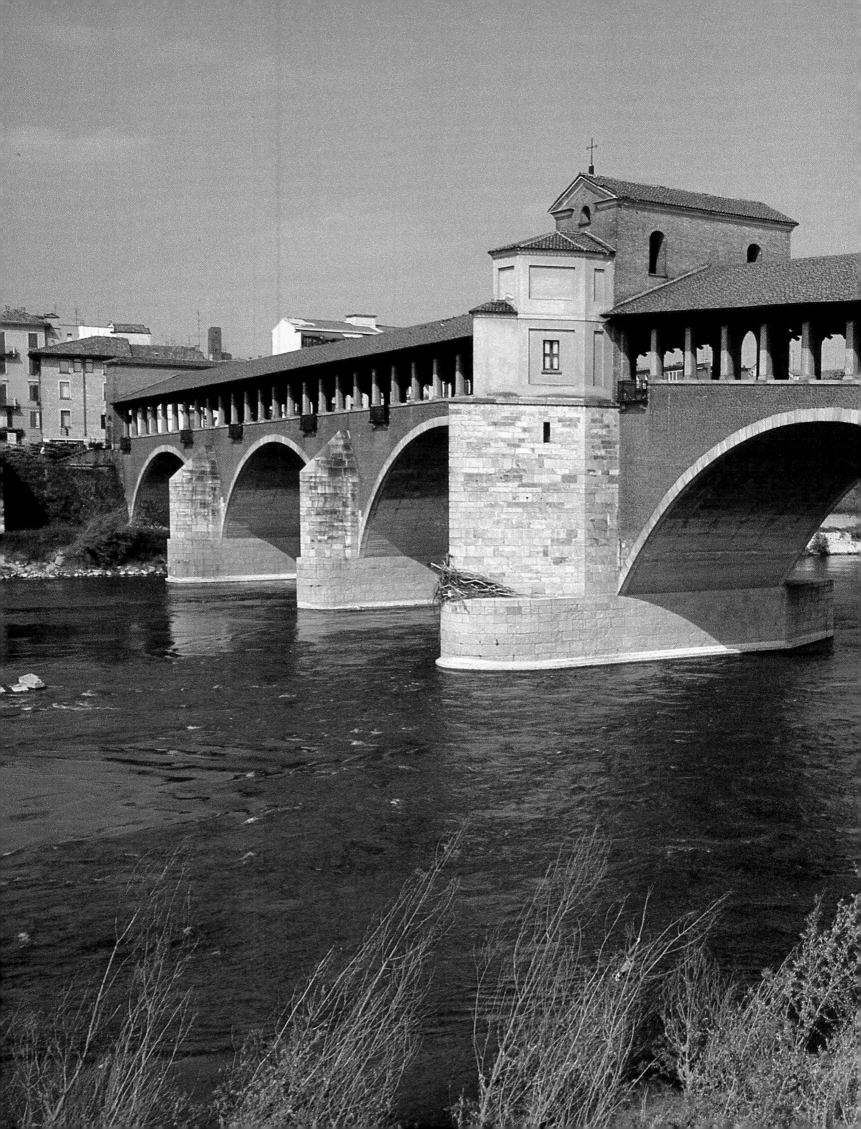

PAVIA

There is no rock in the middle of the plain of the Po, which is why Pavia is completely built of red brick. The city, built on the banks of the river Ticino a little to the north of where it flows into the great Italian river, is distinguished in history as a stronghold, but also as a seat of culture. Still today, hordes of students fill the streets and squares of the town, in the tradition of a university founded in the 11th century and whose benches knew Petrarch and Leonardo da Vinci. The latter, furthermore, collaborated with Bramante in drawing up the plans for Pavia Cathedral, a brick Duomo surmounted by one of the largest cupolas on the pensinsula.

As in Milan, which is not far away, the governments of the Viscontis and the Sforzas left their mark on Pavia. These two great families worked successively to try to complete the jewel of Renaissance Lombardy which is the charterhouse of Pavia. A masterpiece of a monastery, situated in a secluded part of the town, this shrine also contains a mausoleum. Celebrated people lie here, such as Ludovic the Moor, Béatrice d'Este and Gian Galeazzo Visconti. The best artists continued to decorate the charterhouse until the end of the 18th century, making it one of Italy's major monuments. It is difficult to know which to admire most – the 'symphony of marbles' of its facade or the extraordinarily-fashioned decorations of its arches.

Previous pages: The covered bridge of Pavia.

Opposite page: The cathedral.
Top and above: The charterhouse.

33

LOMBARDY

Brescia is situated on the edge of the Lombardy plain at the foot of the Alpine passes, routes of communication since time immemorial, illustrated by the mysterious engraved rocks of the Val Carmonica. The city still retains the lozenge-shaped plan of the Roman camp of its first Golden Age, and spreads from the shelter of a medieval citadel which calls itself the 'Falcon of Italy'. Despite this, the city has long

cafés where the locals gather. The first is the imposing mass of the Broletto, ancient communal palace in Romantic style, flanked by a square tower, and bearing on its facade the elegant Balcony of Proclamations. Next to it is the Duomo Nuovo of the 17th, 18th and 19th centuries, which couples a marble facade inspired by antiquity to a generous modern cupola. Because of its proportions, this shrine literally overshadows its neighbour, the ad-

Top: Rock engravings in Val Camonica.
Above, right and opposite page: The piazza Del Duomo in Brescia.

Following pages: The Marmolada massif in the Dolomites.

forgotten the clamour of battle, although the inhabitants are noted for their rather turbulant nature. This attractive impetuosity is actually part of the charm of a visit to Brescia because most of the town's monuments are in the proximity of the centre.

It is most unusual to see side by side three edifices of the importance of those which constitute the east side of the piazza del Duomo, opposite

mirable Duomo Vecchio, a Roman edifice which is also known as the Rotunda because the curve of its facade is reminiscent of an amphitheatre. The most remarkable thing about this edifice is its 18th century crypt, comsisting of three apses and five aisles, the columns and capitals of which were obtained from ancient Roman monuments.

THE DOLOMITES

The Dolomites is the name given to the Alps which cover a vast region of Northern Italy inland of Venice. The originality of their shapes testify to the type of limestone from which they are formed. This is dolomite, named in honour of Dolomieu, the French geologist who in the 18th century became the first scientist to study the massif. This scholar explained how by attacking differently the two components of the rock, erosion had created the wonderful reliefs where the vertical reigns. Tours, walls, domes and spires were formed in this way above the slopes of gentler shape, covered in forests, alpine meadow and cultivation; the peaks reflected in the torrents, rivers and lakes. The Dolomites rarely rise above an height of three thousand metres, the highest point in the chain being 3,342 m.

A cable-car allows an approach to this summit which reveals one of the most beautiful panoramas of the Alps – and one of the most popular. Tourism is actually the principal activity in the Dolomites, the beauties of which were brought to the attention of the world during the winter Olympic Games which were organized around the three elegant ski-resorts of Cortina d'Ampezzo. Paradise for skiers, alpinists and hikers, the massifs are also an extraordinary natural conservatory for flora and fauna which are preserved in many regional natural parks. Crossed for a long time by itinerant merchants, the Dolomites today have an excellent network of roads which allow the appreciation of their charms from the comfort of vehicles.

VERONA

In Verona, after Venice the most beautiful city of Venetian art, as often as not it is not the treasures of Antiquity, the Middle Ages or the Renaissance which are the first thing visitors want to see, but the very simple balcony of a modest Gothic palace on the via Capello. Forever this town, nestling in a bend in the river Adige, will be the backcloth to the romantic tragedy of Romeo and Juliet and the balcony that to their second meeting after the ball. It is believed that the facts of the legend are based on the historic rivalry between the Montagus and the Capulets, in other words the Guelphs and Ghibellines.

The most beautiful part of the monumental inheritance of Verona comes from a third family, the Scaligers, who governed the town before the Venetian domination and under whom it knew its most prosperous period. At the end of the

Above and opposite page left: The piazza dei Signori.
Right: Piazza delle Erbe.
Opposite page, top: The main entrance of the church of Saint Zenon. Middle: The Communal Palace.

Piazza dei Signori, which also passes the 17th-century Communal Palace, is the Palace of Government which until the end of the 13th century served as the residence of the seigneurs who preceded the Venetian First Magistrates. The presence of the latter is confirmed in the other beautiful esplanade of Verona, the Piazza delle Erbe, where a winged lion, symbol of Venice, is enthroned on the column of San Marco. These monuments include the Gothic mausoleums which the Scaligers built between their palace and their church and this famous family was also responsible for the building of the bridge of brick and marble which crosses the Adige at the Old Castle.

PADUA

In much the same way as in Verona under the Scaligers, Padua reached its high point at the end of the 14th century under the government of the seigneurs of Carrara. It then came under the domination of the Republic of Venice for four centuries. Though the city maintained its prosperity, it was particularly noted for living up to its nickname the "Learned". This was thanks to the renown of its university, where Ga-

with Donatello bronzes. It was this same artist who made the equestrian statue of Gattamelata which can be seen in front of this shrine.

Not far away, near the oval of the Prato della Valle, rise similar cupolas. These belong to the church of Saint Justine, whose riches include a Veronese alterpiece. On the subject of riches, it is a shrine of modest dimensions which demands our attention, the chapel of the Scrovegnis, built in 1303. Giotto

lileo was one of the masters. Dante and Petrarch were among its most famous students.

Today, it is to a very ancient person that Padua pays homage. A good number of its visitors are the pilgrims who come to honour the memory of Saint Anthony. The scene of their fervour is the saint's basilica, whose Byzantine cupolas bring to mind those of the San Marco in Venice. The high altar is decorated

created some of his best work on these walls. The collection of thirty eight frescos are enlivened with an unparalleled mystical power.

Mention should also be made of Andrea Mantegna who, two centuries later, also left his mark on Paduan painting.

Top: frescos by Giotto in The chapel of the Scrovegnis.
Above: The trees in the Prato della Valle.
Opposite page: The domes of the basilica of Saint Justine.

THE VENETO

The Euganei hills which mark Padua's southern horizon were originally volcanic, which explains the abundance of thermal spas in the region. Among them is Abano Terme, renowned for its mud baths to the point of being one of the most frequented thermal spas on the continent. The Romans already appreciated the blessings of this area and realized the true value of the wines nourished by the volcanic soil.

These hills have also been long appreciated simply because of the harmony of their setting. One regular visitor was Petrarch who chose to retire to a hill known today as Arquà Petrarca, where romantics come in pilgrimage to his tomb. People less renowned, but very rich, chose to live in the Euganei hills and they have bequeathed superb estates, such as the Villa Emo and the Villa Barbarigo, to the area.

For their summer palaces, however, the Venetian aristocracy preferred the Brenta Riviera, situated along thirty kilometres of the canalised river after its descent from the Dolomites. Here more than a hundred and twenty villas compete in elegance and again we can imagine an epoch where among the fireworks, nocturnal fêtes echoed to the music of Vivaldi and Cimarosa. The most admirable houses are in the Palladio style, such as the Villa Foscari, and range from the most immense palaces to the discretest residence, like the Villa Sorenzo, whose facade was painted by the brother of Veronese.

Opposite page and below: The Villa Sorenzo, its facade painted by the brother of Veronese. Bottom: The Euganei mountains.

VENICE

What necessity drove the first Venetians to come and establish themselves in such a lagoon? And what a challenge it was for them to build here and establish their maritime glory and their palaces on shifting foundations. In any event, here, at the meeting point of the Orient and Occident, they made their city into a mythical place, drenched today in the inheritance of a prestigious past, but a city which has never ceased to be a beacon of culture for Italy, if not the whole of Europe.

Its images are familiar throughout the world; the gondolas rocking beneath the sun, the pigeons flying above the square of San Marco, the Rialto Bridge spanning the Grand Canal and the shimmering carnival costumes; Venice maintains all that she had to be proud of in the era of the Doges. The power of the republic extended directly throughout the Adriatic, and very quickly, too, through the mediation of merchants to whom Marco Polo opened the way.

This commercial hegemony brought immense riches which Venice dedicated to its embellishment. The greatest architects were invited to work in the lagoon, together with the best artists, musicians, sculptors and painters, the last constituting a school of painting. The names of Titian, Veronese, Tintoretto and Canaletto, suffice to indicate its importance.

It is ironic, really, that a city which for six centuries celebrated with great pomp its marriage to the sea, suffers a little more each year from the rising waters...

Opposite page, top left: Carnival costume. Top right: The Grand Canal in Venice. Middle: Venice at night. Above: A palace on the Grand Canal. Left: The celebrated gondolas.

FRIULI
VENEZIA GIULIA

In the north-east of Italy, towards the frontiers of Austria and Slovenia, Friuli-Venezia Giulia is an administrative region created by special statute which realigns lands long subject to the whims of history and inhabited by peoples of many minorities. There is no obvious geographical unity – the region descending from Alpine summits down through limestone outcrops to a coastal plain fringed by lagoons.

The Adriatic coast lends itself to seaside tourism, as shown by the resorts of Lignano Sabbiadoro and Grado. The latter is very picturesque and, moreover, is an active fishing port. It was built in the lagoon, somewhat in the manner of Venice, by its ancient inhabitants and those of neighbouring Aquileia, who thought by doing so they could escape barbarian invasions. After troubled times this ancient Roman colony recovered its prosperity, notably exemplified by its superb Roman basilica.

The two principle cities of the region are Udine, in the interior, and Trieste, on the coast. Famous for its Gothic and Renaissance monuments, Udine is built around the Piazza della Libertà. Trieste is a modern seaport which has grown up around an historic quarter containing Roman and medieval monuments. The charm of the Trieste Riviera has long been appreciated, as the Miramare chateau, which was built for Archduke Maximilian of Austria, proves.

Opposite page: A basilica in Venezia-Giulia.
Top: The port of Grado.
Middle: Trieste.
Left: The piazza della Libertà in Udine.

49

BOLOGNA AND THE EMILIA-ROMAGNA

The Roman Emilian Way inspired the name 'Emilia', a region which merges the modern epoch with the Roman and which extends to the east and south of Bologna, the main city of the region. Major crossroad of Northern Italy and the country's undisputed gastronomic capital, Bologna has always been of considerable commercial importance, an importance which is reinforced today by a wide range of industrial activities. But Bologna has also flourished during all the various intellectual and artistic movements. The city is proud of the fact that it has one of the oldest universities in Europe while its school of painting was one of the highlights of the 16th century. Bologna's symbolic monument, the famous Fountain of Neptune carved by the sculptor John of Bologna, also dates from this period.

Above: The Fountain of Neptune.
Right: The facade of the abbey of Pomposa.
Opposite page, top: The Communal Palace. Below: The 'trepponti' of Comacchio.

The Renaissance flourished no less brilliantly in Ferrara, a city lying nearby on the plain of the River Po. Behind the protection of its ramparts, now transformed into public gardens, the city still seems rooted in its past. For a long time Ferrara was ruled by the Este family, who bequeathed the city a multitude of artistic treasures and fine architecture, among which are the cathedral, the Este castle and numerous family palaces, edifices now transformed into museums of art.

On a less noble scale, but vividly colourful, Emilia Romagna possesses in Comacchio a most original city. Built on a group of thirteen islands in the ancient delta of the Po, this town of eel fishers is, in effect, divided by its canals crossed by numerous bridges, including the curious Trepponti bridge which dates from 1634.

PARMA

Ancient capital of the Farnesi, who promoted literature and the arts, in later times Parma again flourished artistically, first under the protection of the Bourbons and then ex-Empress Marie-Louise of Austria. The city still cultivates the memory of Correggio and Parmigianino, famous artists of the 16th century, while in music the 19th and 20th centuries witnessed the birth of Verdi and Toscanini.

Whatever else they do, visitors to Parma should not miss the episcopal centre based around an impressive Romanesque cathedral which stands next to a Gothic campanile. Behind the sanctuary is the Baroque church of Saint John the Evangelist which contains Correggio's superb frescos. Next to the Duomo there is an octagonal baptistery, also of rich external appearance. It has facades of sculpted pink marble figures and rhythmic colonnades. The interior has painted embellishments, notably in the cupola. Nearby are the collections of the pharmacy which the Benedictines of Saint John the Evangelist founded in the 9th century. The buildings, restored in the 16th century, also house remarkable frescos.

The Parmigianino heritage can be admired in the Pilotta palace, a huge edifice which houses the National Museum of Antiquities, the Art Museum, the Farnese Theatre, the Palatine Library and the Bodini Museum. The Garden Palace and the beautiful ducal park surrounding it, which were bequeathed by Marie-Louise, once Duchess of Parma, is another tourist rendezvous.

Opposite page: The cathedral of Parma.
Top: The baptistery beside the Duomo.
Above: The church of Saint John the Evangelist.
Left: Its pharmacy.

Above: The basilica of Saint Apollinaire.
Right: Baptistery and campanile.
Opposite page, top: The picture gallery. Below: The arch of the choir of the basilica of Saint Apollinaire.

Previous pages: The dome of the church of Saint Vital.

RAVENNA

At first sight, Ravenna does not appear to live up to the greatness of its reputation. Situated between the sea and the marshlands in the indeterminate landscape of the plain of Romagna, the city has a provincial character and its brick monuments, such as the Municipal Art Gallery, would not have any particular grandeur were they not clad with facades of marble. Ancient capital of the Occidental Empire, beneficiary of the good works of Galla Placidia and Theodorus and later seat of the Viceroy of the Byzantine Empire, Ravenna has known three periods of extraordinary splendour. Far from being ostentatious, Ravenna's rich past dazzlingly reveals itself only when the vistor enters one of the many sanctuaries and mausoleums which sprinkle the city. The glorious colours and symbolism of the mosaics are witness to the spirituality of the early centuries of Christendom. In this unparalleled collection, the mosaics with golden stars beneath the heavens in the mausoleum of Galla Placidia, the most ancient in Ravenna, and those which ornament the apse of the impressive church of Saint Vital are particularly admirable.

The Orthodox baptistery and that of the Aryans also contain beautiful, highly contrasting, mosaics and one should not miss those of the archiepiscopal chapel. Finally, a short distance south of Ravenna, one should see the triumphal arch and the choir cupola of the basilica of Saint Apollinaire in Classe, which represents Christ the Saviour and the Transfiguration.

RIMINI AND SAN MARINO

The renown of the Romagna Riviera is closely linked with that of Rimini, whose fine beaches, yacht harbour and tourist facilities are highly regarded. This elegant resort has been developed on the edge of a city which has ancient roots and which is situated at the intersection of the Emilia and Flaminia Roman roads. After prospering under the Empire, Ariminum became famous in the 13th century under the rule of Malatesta, whose bloody deeds were chronicled by Dante in his Divine Comedy. The monuments in Rimini's ancient heart – the Arch of Augustus, The Bridge of Tiberius and the Temple of Malatesta – recall these two epochs. Inland from the coast, the tiny Repu-

blic of San Marino lies in an incomparable position on the slopes of Mount Titano. Not content with being the smallest republic in the world, San Marino is also the oldest, being founded in the 4th century by the devout stonemason to which it owes its name. There are three castles – the Roca, the Cesta and the Montale – linked by a ring road, on the ridges of Mount Titano, with offer magnificent views of the Apennines, the Romagna countryside, the resorts, the plain of the Po and, in the distance, the lagoon of Venice and the Dalmatian plain. The other eagle's nest of the region is San Leo, an ancient historic village, surmounted by a citadel in which the Count of Cagliostro died in captivity.

Above: San Leo, where the Count of Cagliostro died in captivity. Opposite page, top: A beach at Rimini. Below: The church of San Leo.

TUSCANY

Tuscany, so well praised by Gabriele d'Annunzio and a thousand poets, is Italy at its most sublime; a harmonious world of hills offering a diversity of views and small plains bathed in soft Mediterranean light. A world where man has made his home quite naturally for thousands of years, this region derived its name from that of the Etruscans, the most famous of its inhabitants of yesteryear. They and their descen-

added to the riches of the earth already exploited in the past, such as the celebrated marble of Carrara and the iron pyrites of the Metalliferre mountains. Agriculture is specialized; flowers near Pescia, fruit trees in the river basins, market gardens along the Arno and, above all, the viticulture of Chianti to the south of Florence.

But if wine is one of the most reputable of the products of Italy, it should not be forgotten that Tusca-

Top and right: Wine-sampling in the Tuscany cellars.
Above: The vineyards of Chianti.
Opposite page: The vineyards of Montalcino.

Following pages: The basilica and the Tower of Pisa.

dants constructed an admirable landscape where vineyards, cornfields and olive groves overlap each other, where farmhouses and fine villas gaze from one summit to another or hide behind the rows of cypress trees.

So, at least, is the traditional appearance of a region which modern economics is transforming little by little. The lignite and the geo-thermal energy of Larderello have been

ny as a whole is a paradise for lovers of grand crus. Among the best are the brunello of Montalcino, the muscatel of Sienna, the vernaccia of San Gimignano and the aleatico of Portoferraio.

PISA

Discovering the prodigious monuments which make Pisa one of the great tourist attractions in the world is rather like embracing in a single glance the destiny of this city on the banks of the Arno. Pisa, which has Ligurian, Etruscan, Greek and Roman influences, hardly distinguished itself before the 11th century. Then it openly announced its maritime ambitions and the city quickly became a competitor to Genoa and Venice. Trade with the Western Mediterranean and North Africa, as well as crusades to the Orient, brought considerable prosperity to the city, as its great monuments proves. But its spirit was clearly quenched when the Pisans lost all their fleet at the battle of Meloria, fought against the Genoans in 1294.

Honour where honour is due, on entering the Piazza del Duomo it is the Tower of Pisa that is first investigated thoroughly. The pronounced lean which has given it worldwide fame is a result of the marshy nature of the ground along the Arno and neither the architects of the past nor modern technicians have succeeded in halting its slow sinking till quite recently. The pure Romance style of the bell tower is not representative of Pisan art; the nearby cathedral is the best example of that. One admires the rhythmic facade of pure and sombre marbles, and the contrasting studies of the play of light and shadow in the colonnaded galleries. In front of the Duomo, complementing its exceptional structure, is a baptistery, similarly decorated.

FLORENCE

".. and I have discovered from afar, like a sombre mass, Santa Maria del Fiore and its famous dome, Brunelleschi's masterwork. It is there that Dante, Michelangelo and Leonardo da Vinci lived!" Today, one can again discover Florence with Stendahl's eyes and before the face of this prestigious city – in itself sufficient to sum up all the genius of Italy – one is overcome by what is almost timidity. Where must one begin?

From history we learn that Florence was founded by Caesar as a fort to guard the Via Flaminia where it crossed the river Arno. It was to be a thousand years before the city become the capital of Tuscany and began to prosper by virtue of its merchants and its craftsmen in wool and silk, organized into powerful corporations. They were supported by the Florentine bankers, inventors of the florin, a gold coin which was quickly accepted internationally. Internal struggles between the Ghibellines and the Guelphs did not spare Florence, but the city profited nonetheless from the beneficial influence of the Medici in business and in the arts. In this family, the figure of Lorenzo the Magnificent stands out. In his enlightened patronage he was the incarnation of the spirit of the Renaissance. He ruined the family bank but made Florence the intellectual capital of the West, a city governed until the 18th century by the Medici, who continued to support art in all its forms. Is it surprising, therefore, that Florence is a city where there is always something new to discover?

FLORENCE

Legacy of the first Roman bridge, which was not far away over the same narrows of the river Arno, the Ponte Vecchio is one of the oldest monuments of Florence. Its half-open little jewellery shops, one next to another, gives a good picture of the city's medieval period. This work of art is surmounted by a gallery which allowed princes to pass discreetly from the Pitti Palace, a Renaissance edifice on the left bank, to the Palazzo Vecchio, a severe Gothic construction on the opposite bank. This palace was renovated in the 16th century and it is its bell tower that rises above the Piazza della Signoria with its famous Fountain of Neptune. To make the crossing pleasant, this Palatine Gallery was used as an exhibition gallery for works of art collected by the Medici, so being the origin of the Uffizi Gallery.

In strong contrast to the severity of

Above and right: The Ponte Vecchio.
Opposite page, top left: Statue in front of the Old Palace.
Top right: The Fountain of Neptune.
Middle: Detail of the campanile.

Previous pages: A general view of Florence.

the Palazzo Vecchio the momumental unity of the Piazzo del Duomo, in the heart of Florence, is one of the best possible visions of the New Age, whose coming was due to the patronage of the Medici. Here, in this superb symphony of white, green and pink marble, the Renaissance expresses the ideals of refinement and culture which so animated the Florentines in the times of the Medici. In its dimensions and richness of its decoration, moreover, the cathedral reflects the opulence of the city – though judging from the elegance of the nearby baptistery, this was no less great during the Romantic period. The bronze doors and mosaics of the cathedral are particularly famous.

SIENNA

Ancient rival of Florence, city of the arts and of the past, the perfection of Sienna has remained intact behind its walls, rusty-ochre as its earth. Situated on three hills, in the shadow of two instantly-recognisable towers, the city does not slumber in the glories of its past, for the university and its students ensure a very lively atmosphere the whole year round. As far as pleasure goes, all records are broken during the annual recalling the Government of Nine of the period of Sienna's greatest prosperity in the 13th and 14th centuries. Indeed, it was after the defeat of Florence at the battle of Montaperti in 1260 that Sienna entered its golden age. The city's ambitions can be measured by the substantial development of the ramparts, which the merchant houses of the city never succeeded in completing. Neither did Sienna, the city of Saint Bernadine and of Saint Catherina,

Opposite page: Assembling for the Palio festival at the foot of the Torre del Mangia.
Left and bottom right: The costumes for this annual manifestation.
Below: The statue of Bandini.

festival of Palio, a traditional horse race in which ten of the seventeen quarters of the city compete and which is accompanied by colourful processions, recalling the splendour of yesteryear.

Famous far beyond the frontiers of Italy, this event takes place at the foot of the tall Torre del Mangia, in the piazza del Campo, a remarkable pedestrian precinct in the form of a shell. Its paving is in nine sections patron saint of Italy, succeed in fully finishing its cathedral. Despite this, the 13th century Duomo can be greatly admired for its rich facade, the originality of its light and dark marble panoply and its paving of inlaid marble.

SAN GIMIGNANO

In the centre of Tuscany, above the smiling valley of the Elsa, a series of thirteen medieval towers make the silhouette of San Gimignano unique. These are only a few of the house-towers which covered the city in the 12th and 13th centuries. This abundance was a reflection of the rivalries between the great families of the city, variations on the theme of the struggles between the Guelphs and Ghibellines, which fi-nally resulted in San Gimignano falling into a state of decadence. In 1353, it came under the guardian-ship of Florence.

Today's visitor can only be happy that this decline occurred because it allowed the city to retain its medie-val atmosphere. The piazza della Cisterna still centres around a 13th-century well which looks out on the austere facades and the noble to-wers of its time, the walls and roofs all clothed with the famous ochre of

Above: San Gimignano.
Right: The environs of San Gimignano.
Opposite page: The abbey of Monte Oliveto Maggiore and the Tuscan countryside.

Tuscany, gilded by the evening sun. And in this majesty, the same ambiance bathes the piazzo del Duomo, which encloses the collegiate church with a series of palaces and square towers.

In San Gimignano, Tuscany matches the harmony of the natural environment and the richness of its heritage in a most remarkable manner. The same can be said – to a lesser extent – of the Abbey of Monte Oliveto Maggiore which is found nestling among seductive hills, surrounded by cypress trees. The pearl of this abbey is its great cloister which is decorated with superb frescos dating from the beginning of the 16th century.

ASSISI AND UMBRIA

Lying between Tuscany, the Marches and Latium, Umbria is unusual in that it does not have one kilometre of coastline and lies completely away from the main traffic routes. This accounts for the peaceful nature, unpretentious and timeless, of this 'green heart' of Italy where Piero della Francesca, Raphael or Fra Angelico loved to paint the light.

This land where life is sweet is site of the very popular festival of the Two Worlds; and Gubbio, famous for its ceramics.

Enclosed within its medieval walls, Gubbio is graced by noble towers, a palace and sanctuaries containing precious frescos, and is distinguished for its original traditional festivals.

The highest place of all in Umbria, lying on a foothill of Mount Subasio, Assisi lives on in the memory of Saint Francis whose spiritual mes-

Opposite page: The Carceri hermitage, hollowed out of the rock.
Below: The basilica of Saint Francis of Assisi.
Bottom right: Gubbio, celebrated for its ceramics.

sprinkled with cities of famous name, situated in dominating positions above the river basins and valleys. One of these is Perugia, capital city of the region, famous for its painters, notably Perugino who was Raphael's master. The most important monuments of Perugia are grouped around the famous piazza 4 November.

High-lying, too, are Orvieto, papal city with its surprising cathedral; Spoleto, whose ancient walls are the

sage was ideally depicted by Cimabue and Giotto. Their frescos, whose style is highly realistic and powerfully evocative and which broke with Italian aesthetics, cover the walls of the Saint Francis Basilica. Those who wish to approach Saint Francis of Assisi more directly must go to one of the hermitages where he loved to meditate, such as that in Carceri, where the sanctuary is hollowed out of the rock.

THE MARCHES

The Marches (from the German 'marken' = frontier) got this name because once they marked the limits of the Papal States and the empire of the Franks, and because of its geographically central position between two very different areas, that of the north reminiscent of Romagna, that of the south already heralding the Abruzzi.

Many towns have established a presence in the Marches, first and foremost Ancona, the capital. This is a port which has never ceased its activities since the days of the Greeks of Syracuse and which once even put itself forward as a rival to Venice. Many notable monuments recall this past, particularly the cathedral dedicated to Saint Cyriac, patron saint of places, whose 12-sided dome is one of the oldest in Italy. Ancona also possesses charming edifices such as the famous Fountain of the Calamo dating from 1560.

Other towns of importance in the Marches are Loreto, spiritual home of pilgrims who come from all over the world to venerate the Holy Chest miraculously transported from Nazareth; Fermo, centre of art and culture, charmingly nestling between sea and land; and finally Urbino, birthplace of Raphael. He was born in 1483 at the end of the reign of Federico da Montefeltro who had made his town a haven of peace for artists. Today, Urbino still exudes an atmosphere of serenity, as though it were still under the protection of the superb ducal palace, where the famous collections assembled by the local ruler benefit from incomparable surroundings.

Opposite page, top: The Duomo of the cathedral of Ancona. Middle: Urbino, the birthpace of Raphael. Above: The port of Ancona. Left: The Calamo fountain.

THE ABRUZZI

Around the Gran Sasso which reaches a height of almost 3000 metres and constitutes the highest region of the Apeninne chain, the Abruzzi, like neighbouring Calabria, are a region of barren appearance with a raw climate and contrasting landscapes. The high Sangro valley has been established as a national park for the protection of eagles, Abruzzi wolves, bears and wild cats as well as many chamois and deer.

To the north, in the environs of the Corno Grande, the Gran Sasso massif has winter sports centres much appreciated by modern-day Romans. Composed of limestone, these mountains often have an air of grandeur and highly-appreciated routes include, for example, the gorges of Vomano and Sagitario near the Great Plateaux. Summer tourism in the Abruzzi, however, is still largely based on the seaside resorts on the Adriatic coast.

Behind its seeming deprivation, the Abruzzi are proud of their historic cities and a past full of grandeur. It is the medieval city of Sulmona that guards the memory of the poet Ovid in superb natural surroundings. It is Pescasseroli which saw the birth of the philosopher Benedetto Croce or Bominaco and Corfinio with their remarkable sanctuaries. It is, above all, L'Aquila, where the legend of Saint Bernadine of Sienna, who died there in 1444, is cultivated by means of a surprising fountain with 99 pipes and where at the same time her memory is honoured.

Her mausoleum is in a beautiful 16th century basilica which has been added to the most harmonious Roman basilica of Santa Maria di Collemaggio.

Above: The Gran Sasso which is almost 3,000 m. high.
Opposite page top left: The Roman basilica of Santa Maria de Collemaggio.

NAPLES

Voluble, querulous, insufferable, disarming, the Neopolitans themselves are the first object of interest in Naples, and it is not surprsing that this city cultivated, if not invented, the opera seria, the opera buffa and the commedia dell'arte. It is fortunate that its people complement the city so well, because Naples does not always present itself in a flattering light. Dogged by its bad reputation, not truly coquettish, traversed by broad highways full of demented traffic or criss-crossed by unattractive alleyways, it seems that Naples cannot compete with the grandeur of the extraordinary bay which opens before the quaysides of its harbour.

The beauty of Naples as a city is not flagrant, it is true, but many of its vistas are very seductive. A good example is the harbour of Santa Lucia and the dell'Ovo castle, made popular by the most famous of all Neopolitan songs.

This is also true of the Carthusian monastery of Saint Martin, which can be discovered on a spur of Vomero mountain. Beneath the castle of Saint Elmo, with its beautiful Baroque church and its attendant museum, whose most notable exhibits are the touching Neopolitan cribs, this monastery is the epitome of the patrimony of the metropolis of southern Italy.

Naples is indeed rich in castles and palaces, but even more so in churches and Baroque monuments as well as museums which are regarded as being among the most interesting in the country. This is particularly true of the national archeological museum whose collections are derived from the Farnese family and from intriguing relics excavated at Pompeii and Herculaneum.

Opposite page: The piazza Victor-Emmanuel II.
Below: General view of Naples.
Bottom: The port of Naples.

Above and right: Ischia, largest island in the Gulf of Naples. Opposite page: The sea around Capri.

THE GULF OF NAPLES AND ITS ISLANDS

To 'see Naples and die', as the saying goes, it is necessary to distance oneself so that the great city with Mount Vesuvius at its back and Mount Faito on its flank can be truly admired. That is to say that one must embark for the islands in the bay. These are three in number, each enjoying an unequal fame. To the greatest joy of lovers of peace and calm, the little island of Procida has remained off the tourist route, although its beaches are attractive and the lifestyle of its fishermen, farmers and winegrowers does not lack originality. The neighbouring island of Ischia, in contrast, is the largest in the Gulf of Naples. The interior is a land of farmers, of the white-housed villages of winegrowers, of olive groves and with a generally abundant vegetation. Around this, the pine forests descend to the slopes above the turquoise waves and a few ports scattered along the coast, such as Sant'Angelo. Lastly, the capital is in two parts: Ischia Porto, dominated by its Castello, and Ischia Ponte, with its colourful houses.

In Capri, which lies off the peninsula of Sorrento, one sets foot on an island of all the excesses. It is the marine resort par excellence, whose panoramic views outstrip the greatest in the world, judging by the waves of tourist who come here. The miracle is that Capri has remained itself; elegant in the image of its operetta capital, evocative to those who marvel at the villa Jovis of the Emperor Tiberius, savage in its reefs, such as the Faraglioni, steep cliffs and caves, such as the legendary Blue Grotto.

VESUVIUS

Its silhouette rising baldly above the Bay of Naples, Vesuvius sleeps lightly, spitting fumaroles to remind one of its last eruption, as recently as 1944. Every town in its vicinity has been buried several times under the ashes of the illustrious volcano, notably Torre Annunziata and Torre de Greco. But not all is bad in its choleric eruptions, judging by the manner in which the fruit orchards and the vines which produce 'Lacryma Christi' climb the lower slopes of the mountain.

At the rim of the crater of dizzying steepness, the courageous visitor becomes conscious of the might of volcanic forces, and this excursion is a good introduction to the discovery of the dead cities of Pompeii and Herculaneum. Both disappeared in a few hours after Vesuvius erupted on August 24th in the seventy-ninth year of our era.

Herculaneum was buried under

waves of mud which petrified the town without consuming it. Pompeii was buried under a rain of red hot volcanic ash.

The vestiges of the past are nonetheless extremely interesting because daily life was rich and lively at the time of the cataclysm. Commencing in the 18th century, the excavations of Pompeii have revealed an instantaneous drama, bodies frozen in expectation of death. But, in particular, they have also re-vealed the refinement of Roman civilization in the days of the Empire, as witnessed by the silver vessels, delicate frescos, mosaics, gardens filled with statues, the beakers, for example those of the house of the Vettii.

Top: The House of the Vettii.
Above: The ampitheatre of Pompeii.
Opposite page, middle: Vesuvius.
Opposite page, bottom: A fountain.

Above: Attrani.

Opposite page: Vineyards and

terraces along the Amalfi coast.

THE AMALFI COAST

Enclosing the Bay of Naples to the south, the escarpments of the Sorrento peninsula knew an early predilection for seaside resorts which then spread to Amalfi and its coastline. The original tourism, both chic and British, transformed the tiny fishing ports into elegant resorts, linked by a spectacular corniche. There, as is the case all along the Amalfi coast, the traditional environment has survived between the villas, and one can still see the olive, lemon and orange groves and vineyards climbing the slopes.

Between Sorrento and Salerno, Amalfi reigns over a coastline which is said to be without rival on the peninsula. This coast alternates between fantastically shaped rocks, plunging into the sea, savage gorges, their slopes clothed in luxurious vegetation, and fishing villages clinging for better or worse above the inlets. Amalfi itself is a picturesque and acrobatic town famous for being the first of Italy's maritime republics, having been founded in 840. It maintained a flourishing trade with Constantinople, which can be seen from the eastern influences of its cathedral of Saint Andrea. This sanctuary is dedicated to the saint whose relics it contains.

The other village resorts, such as Positano, Vettica Maggiore, Atrani and Vietri sul Mare, surround Amalfi and rival its charm. Ravello is one of marvels this coast. Andre Gide wrote of it: "It is closer to heaven than it is to the coast."

THE POUILLE

Apulia, which extends to the spur on the heel of the boot of Italy, is an agricultural region which has known many ages of prosperity. The most remarkable, at the beginning of the 13th century, is associated with the sojourn here of Emperor Frederick II of Souabe. He was a curious character, cruel and atheistic but at the same time a patron and an excellent governor whose son, Manfred, continued his work. After his return

Monte, reached through a gate inspired by antiquity, is decorated in a half-Roman, half-Gothic style, a style which is unusually elegant.

Around d'Alberobello, Apulia consists of a country said to be that of the 'trulli', because the houses there are all so unusual. Trulli are houses with very thick, whitewashed stone walls covered with conical roofs. It is thought that it was a people who came from the Orient who introduced this technique, inherited from

Above, right and below:
The remarkable stone houses in
Trulli country.
Opposite page: Castel del Monte.

from the crusades, the Emperor had innumerable fortified places constructed in Italy, but he gave Apulia an edifice unique of its kind, the Castel del Monte. Upright and solitary on a hill in the Murge mountains in the province of Bari, this mighty castle served as his summer residence and a hunting lodge. It is built in the form of an octogon, with eight towers, also octagonal in shape, at the corners, the solid armour which protected a sovereign first friend, then enemy, of Pope and Islam. The interior of the Castel del

Neolithic times, into the region, a technique which has been preserved, scarcely modified, because of its insolation properties.

SICILY, PALERMO AND CEFALU

Very few territories have given rise to so much avarice as Sicily, the key to the Mediterranean and the largest of its islands. From the Greeks to the Bourbons of Naples, including the Arabs and the Normans, every occupant has left its mark on Sicily's soil, while the original Sicilians cultivated their own identity and perfected the art of resistance to authority.

Their manner, a mixture of malice and quiet discretion, even silence, make the Sicilians rather less exuberant than other Italians.

Palermo, the capital of the island, does not open itself very easily, but one can never forget the impression it gives the first time one lays eyes on it. Exotic, picturesque, chaotic and rich in contrasts, Palermo is full of strong images! The heart of the city is formed around two adjacent squares, the Quattro Canti and the

Previous pages: The temple of Segeste in Sicily.
Above: The piazza Pretoria in Palermo.
Right: Cefalù.

Opposite page, top: Inhabitants of Cefalù. Middle: The town between the rocks and the waves.

piazza Pretoria with its monumental 16th-century fountain. The city has many monuments, but perhaps its principal one is the Palace of the Normans, where a wonderful 12th-century Palatine chapel has mosaics which bear comparison with those of Ravenna and Constantinople.

Although short, the occupation of the Normans, particularly in the reign of Roger II, gave Sicily many edifices of original architecture, at the same time Norman, Arabic and Byzantine. One of the most successful examples of this is the cathedral of Cefalù, which also benefitted from its exceptional position between the waves and a huge rock.

SYRACUSE AND TAORMINA

From afar Syracuse is a name which makes men dream. It cannot be ignored that in its days of greatest splendour it rivalled Athens and Carthage and that it was as famous for its tyrants as it was for its poets and scholars, the foremost of which was the genius, Archimedes. From the moment it is revealed, perched on the east coast of Sicily, overlooking a majestic bay, Syracuse fulfils all its promise. And when the moment comes to walk through this ancient garden, it is not necessary to be erudite in order to marvel. Here is the immense Greek theatre, where the Tragedy of Aeschylus was performed for the first time; there is the cave called the 'Ear of Dionysius' where the tyrant spied on his prisoners; then the catacombs and the altar where Hieronymus II practised sacrifices. To finish where it all began, we can admire the illustrious fountain of Arethusa, legendary cradle of Syracuse, in the Città Vecchia which is situated on the island of Ortygia.

In the east of Sicily, under the snowy cone of Mount Etna, also lies the industrious city of Catania, accompanied by a chain of small villages, some of them fishing ports, some seaside resorts. But these cannot compete with the ancient town of Taormina; medieval, romantic and wonderfully constructed on a balcony above the sea. Drowned in exuberant, colourful vegetation, well provided with monuments of every epoch, Taormina is also valued for the marvellous panoramas it offers of the coast and the volcano.

PIAZZA ARMERINA

At the heart of Sicily, Piazza Armerina made its name because of the discovery in its vicinity, between the two world wars, of the Roman villa of Casale. But independent of this monument the little city attracts the eye because of the disposition of its houses which enclose the Duomo on top of a hill in verdant surroundings.

A lazy stroll through the alleys of Piazza Armerina confirms this impression and one comes across several palaces, the recently restored Duomo, which contains interesting works of art, and the church of Saint Peter with its richly panelled ceiling. Moreover, in August the city forms the backcloth to medieval festivals comparable to the Palio of Sienna, with processions and Norman costumes.

The countryside around Piazza Armerina has revealed important ancient remains, such as the Greek city of Morgantina and many villas decorated with mosaics. The most famous of these, the Roman villa of Casale, remarkable for its dimensions, is almost entirely decorated with mosaics. Belonging to a wealthy merchant in the third or fourth century after the birth of Christ, this residence constitutes a quite extraordinary picture of the mores and social life of those times. Most of the mosaics of the Casale villa have retained their lively colours which glisten, for example, in the scene which has been named 'The Chamber of the Young Maidens', while the freshness of the inspiration in illustrated by the gently erotic scene which decorates the bedroom of the master of the house.

Above: Piazza Armerina and the Duomo.
Opposite page: Pleasantly erotic mosaics in the villa of Casale.

*Above: Napoleon's house on the
island of Elba.*
*Above and opposite page, top:
Portoferraio, the capital.*
Opposite page, bottom: 'Capoliven'.

ELBA AND THE SMALL ITALIAN ISLANDS

For Italy, the islands are like the cherry on the cake. Not Sicily and Sardinia, which are almost too extensive to retain their insular dimension, but those which are often ignored, colourful and riddled with tradition. These dozens of islands belong to what might be described as archipelagos, such as the Tremiti opposite the Dalmatian coast, the Pelagia near Tunisia, the Egadi off the western point of Sicily, the Aeolians off the north-east coast of Sicily which include the volcano of Stromboli, or the Pontines at the same latitude as Naples.

With Gorgona, Capraia, Pianosa, Montecristo, Giglio and Giannutri, the Tuscan archipelago also counts among these scatterings of rock and earth. These islands, grouped

around Elba, are evidence of a continent swallowed by the Tyrrhenian Sea. The island of Elba is the only one of respectable size and also the only one to have durably inscribed its name in the annals of history. The island lost its anonimity with Cosimo de Medici, duke of Florence, who created its capital, Portoferraio, nowadays well known as a seaside resort. Elba's finest hour, however, was the ten months Napoleon spent as a prisoner there during his first exile after he had assumed sovereignty. A visit to the island from then on included the villa Napoleon in San Martino and various harbours dotted along the coast, notably Marina di Campo and Porto Azzurro. Nor should one omit to mention the high places, such as Capoliveri, which offer remarkable panoramic views.

Above: A view of sailboats near
Porto Cervo.
Opposite page: The countryside
around Porto Cervo.

SARDINIA

Today Sardinia, whose Costa Smeralda makes every dream come true, has been taken over by lovers of the sun, the sand and water sports. The island, however, has traditionally centred around its interior. Its pastoral and mountain civilization go back to prehistoric times. This land, which has aroused many desires and which has been conquered several times, has always remained suspicious, without ever abandoning its originality. Rebellious yet nonetheless hospitable, of savage beauty yet knowing how to be charming when occasion arises, Sardinia allows various facets of itself to be seen. Lovers of local colour discover here original farmhouse lodgings, hikers trek around the lakes and the peaks of the Gannargentu massif which culminates in the 1830 m high La Marmora. Others, without the least exertion, embark on boats to enjoy the marine grottos, of which Sardinia has many exceptional examples. The natural beauty alternates with man-made constructions which are at least of equal interest. Following the course of history, the nuraghi and the impressive giants' tombs which date from the Bronze Age, then the ancient remains of the city of Tharros offer the best examples. And finally, the Roman and Gothic shrines, influenced by the art of Pisa and Lombardy, yet with a style peculiar to Sardinia. Cagliari, the capital of the island, and Sassari, the second city, should not be neglected, despite their bustling modern appearance, because the folklore displays there are of an exuberance never before experienced.

LATIUM

The crushing presence of Rome and twenty-eight centuries of history are related by the monuments tracing the history of Latium, the cradle of Roman civilization. Without pretending to rival Tuscany or Campania, Latium nonetheless possesses a certain charm, while many high spiritual places define its horizons.

In a remarkable series of abbeys and monasteries, one first examines Fossanova, the most ancient Cistercian foundation in Italy, built in 1133. The abbey and the cloister have retained their original Roman configuration and it is to this haven of serenity that Saint Thomas Aquinus returned in 1274. Belonging to the same Cistercian order, the abbey of Casamari is a little less old, but old enough to be a good example of early Italian Gothic style.

These two monasteries governed by the order of Saint Bernard, are

Above: The monastery of Monte Casino.
Right: The abbey of Casamari.
Opposite page: Castel Gandolfo, summer residence of the Popes.

Following pages: The fountains of the Villa D'Este.

neighbours of the monastery of Montecassino, one of the pillars of Christianity. It was within these walls that Saint Benoit established the Benedictine order in the 6th century. This order was adopted by thousands of religious communities throughout Europe.

The monastery of Montecassino knew its greatest prestige in the 11th century, an epoch in which the monks became masters in the art of the miniature, of frescos and of mosaics. South Latium includes Castel Gandolfo, the ancient Alba Longa, rival of Rome, which the Popes made their summer residence.

THE ROMAN COUNTRYSIDE

Although the monasteries constitute the essential heritage of the southern region of Latium, the countryside around Rome and the north of Latium, in contrast, has many beautiful villas of every genre. A single name, Tivoli, which is known throughout the world, is sufficient to understand the villas in question. In the Roman epoch as in the Renaissance this town with its temperate climat and its environment in the foothills of the Apennines was frequently chosen by Romans in high society who wished to possess a country estate.

The estate of the Villa Hadrian, in Tivoli, was actually a monumental unity without equal in the ancient world. The Emperor, after having travelled all over the Empire, wanted a place where he could assemble his souvenirs and reminders of his journeys in Greece, Asia Minor and Egypt. In an idyllic setting, the ruins of these monuments, scattered among lakes and gardens, constitute an unforgettable tableau.

Tivoli's other jewel is the villa of Cardinal Hippolyte Este, son of Lucretia Borgia, which he had built in 1550. More than its buildings and apartments, though they were the most sumptuous of their time, it is the gardens which have given the Villa D'Este its universal renown. The play of water and the fountains singing in unison, through a pond in the form of a shell atrributed to Bernini, to a 'Rometta' in which are reproduced many monuments of ancient Rome, before one walks into the marvellous street of a Hundred Fountains.

ANCIENT ROME

Civilizations converged on Rome as on other places and few cities are so badly adapted to the automobile. The result is that the first impression one receives of Rome is that of extreme confusion. It is necessary to organise a visit well and a discovery of the city obviously begins with the Roman Forum. In those places which were the centre of the political, religious, economic and social life of the city, the evidence of a dozen centuries lies side by side and it is not easy to recognize the historical order of the Basilica Aemelia, the Curia, the Arch of Septimus Severus, that of Titus and the ten temples or shrines scattered around the area.

Our itinerary takes us along the base of the Palatine, one of the seven hills of Rome, where Romulus and Remus, legendary founders of the city, were suckled by a wolf. We then go to the Arch of Constantine and the overpowering Coliseum and arrive back at an enfilade of Imperial forums dominated by the column of Trajanus. Here is the imposing Capitol, the most symbolic of the hills of Rome, where the church of Santa Maria d'Aracoeli, palaces and gardens are found around a sumptuous square designed by Michelangelo, We can also revisit the past at the Pantheon, a temple transformed into a church in the 7th century and, on the other bank of the Tiber, the Saint Angelo castle, which was originally the mausoleum of Hadrian. Other things a visitor must see are the thermal baths of Caracalla and the catacombs, as well as a legion of antique monuments.

Above: The Saint Angelo castle.

Top: The Capitol.

Opposite page: The Forum.

ROME AND THE VATICAN

The first Rome grew under the Etruscans around a citadel on the Capitol. Then came the Republic, personified by Julius Caesar, and the Empire, controlled by Augustus and his successors, who ruled over the Mediterranean basin. But Rome has never truly been the Eternal City since the coming of Christianity. The capital of the Empire was displaced by Constantinople. Rome remained the papal city, and as such, the beacon of a triumphant Christianity. The sovereign pontiffs found patrons, notably during the Renaissance, and to them Rome owes many of its jewels. Saint Peter's Basilica, the heart of Vatican City, for example, carries the stamp of Bramante, Michelangelo, Bernini and Maderno and this shrine houses some very precious sacred works of art. It was the same with the Papal Palaces, built by one Pope after another, around the recently restored jewel of the Sixtine Chapel, the masterwork of Michelangelo. Three older basilicas accompany Saint Peter's of Rome. These are those of San Giovanni in Laterano, San Paolo fuori le Mura and Santa Maria Maggiore.

The architects and the artists of the Eternal City did not lose their influence after the Renaissance, and the Baroque period was particularly prolific. A single example suffices to show this, the Trevi fountain, one of the triumphs of its genre and which Fellini used as one of the symbols in his film La Dolce Vita.

*Above: Saint Peter's basilica in
Rome, the heart of Vatican city.
Opposite page: The Trevi fountain
turns its back on the palazzo Poli.*

107

CONTENTS

INDEX

PHOTO CREDITS